Gooseberry Patch
hot cocoa
Classics

Animal crackers and cocoa to drink,
That is the finest of suppers, I think.
-Christopher Morley

Lotsa Hot Cocoa

1-1/2 c. sugar
1-1/4 c. baking cocoa
3/4 t. salt
1-3/4 c. hot water

4 qts. milk
1 T. vanilla extract
Garnish: whipped topping,
  marshmallows, cinnamon

Combine sugar, cocoa and salt in a stockpot; gradually add hot water. Bring to a boil over medium heat for 2 minutes, stirring constantly. Pour in milk; heat through but do not boil. Remove from heat; stir in vanilla. Whisk mixture until foamy; serve immediately, garnished as desired. Makes about 24 servings.

A cup of hot cocoa brings out the kid in all of us.
Go ahead...treat yourself!

Choco-Minty Hot Cocoa

3 c. milk, divided   1/8 t. salt
8 small chocolate-covered   1 c. whipping cream
   mint patties, chopped

In a medium saucepan over medium-low heat, combine
1/2 cup milk with mint patties until patties are melted. Stir
until smooth; add salt and remaining milk. Bring to a simmer;
stir in cream. Serves 6.

Make a mug of cocoa extra special with a dollop of
sweetened whipped cream. Beat together 1/2 pint whipping
cream with one tablespoon sugar and one teaspoon vanilla
until soft peaks form. So yummy!

Maple Hot Chocolate

1/4 c. sugar
1 T. baking cocoa
1/8 t. salt
1/4 c. hot water
1 T. butter

4 c. milk
1 t. maple flavoring
1 t. vanilla extract
12 marshmallows, divided

Stir together sugar, cocoa and salt in a medium saucepan over medium heat. Add hot water and butter; bring to a boil. Blend in milk, maple flavoring, vanilla and 8 marshmallows. Heat through, stirring occasionally, until marshmallows have melted. Serve in 4 mugs, each topped with a marshmallow. Makes 4 servings.

Hot Cocoa Nog

1 qt. eggnog
3 c. milk
1/2 c. chocolate syrup

1 T. vanilla extract
1/2 t. nutmeg

Combine eggnog, milk and chocolate syrup in a large saucepan over medium heat. Stir constantly until heated through; add vanilla and nutmeg. Serves 4.

A steaming cup of hot chocolate with buttered toast is surely one of the most heart-warming, body-warming, and taste-satisfying combinations known to man.

-James Beard

Hot Chocolate Supreme

1 c. sugar
1/2 c. baking cocoa
1/4 t. salt
5 c. water
2 c. milk

1 c. whipping cream
Garnish: marshmallows,
   whipped topping,
   crushed peppermint
   candies

Combine sugar, cocoa and salt in a medium saucepan; whisk in water. Bring to a boil over high heat, stirring until sugar is completely dissolved. Reduce heat to medium; add milk and cream. Heat through; keep warm over low heat. Serve topped with marshmallows or whipped topping and sprinkled with crushed peppermint candies. Serves 4 to 6.

Keep beverages warm and always have a napkin handy...wrap them together. Just wrap a napkin around a mug and secure with a napkin ring. Fill the mug with your favorite cocoa...quick & easy!

Old-Fashioned Hot Chocolate

1/3 c. sugar
1/4 c. baking cocoa
1/4 t. salt
3 c. milk, divided
3/4 t. vanilla extract
1 c. whipping cream
1-oz. sq. bittersweet baking
    chocolate, chopped

1-oz. sq. white baking
    chocolate, chopped
3/4 c. whipping cream,
    whipped
2 T. mini semi-sweet
    chocolate chips

Combine sugar, cocoa, salt and 1/2 cup milk in a slow cooker.
Beat until smooth; stir in remaining milk and vanilla. Cover
and cook on low setting for 2 hours. Add whipping cream;
cover and cook on low setting for an additional 10 minutes.
Stir in baking chocolates until smooth. Divide hot chocolate
into 6 mugs; top each with 2 tablespoons whipped cream and
one teaspoon mini chocolate chips. Serves 6.

There will be plenty of rosy cheeks after the kids
go caroling...warm them up with a winter tailgate party.
Serve hot chocolate and lots of homemade cookies,
they'll love it!

Let-It-Snow Cocoa

2 c. whipping cream
6 c. milk
1 t. vanilla extract

12-oz. pkg. white
    chocolate chips

Combine all ingredients in a slow cooker. Cover and cook on low setting for 2 to 2-1/2 hours. Stir well to blend before serving. Makes 10 servings.

Easy Peppermint Marshmallows

3/4 c. powdered sugar
1 t. peppermint extract

10-1/2 oz. pkg. mini
    marshmallows

In a plastic zipping bag, shake together powdered sugar and extract. Add marshmallows and toss to coat. Store in an airtight container. Makes about 5 cups.

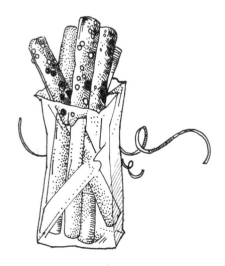

Dip pretzel rods into
melted chocolate
for quick & easy
stirrers.

Mexican Hot Chocolate

6 c. milk, divided
1/2 c. sugar
3 1-oz. sqs. unsweetened
   baking chocolate,
   chopped

1 t. cinnamon
2 eggs, beaten
1 T. vanilla extract
Garnish: whipping cream,
   whipped

Combine one cup milk, sugar, chocolate and cinnamon in a
large saucepan; stir over medium-low heat until chocolate is
melted. Gradually stir in remaining milk. Heat and stir until
very hot; do not boil. Gradually stir hot mixture into eggs, then
return entire mixture to saucepan. Heat and stir for 2 minutes
over low heat. Remove from heat; stir in vanilla and beat with
an electric mixer on medium speed until very frothy. Pour into
mugs; garnish with whipped cream. Makes 6 servings.

Plain china or glass mugs are easy to find. Create a
one-of-a-kind set by adding polka dots, stripes or names
with acrylic permanent paint...it's so easy and clean-up
with water is a breeze.

French Hot Chocolate

2 to 3 1-oz. sqs.
   unsweetened baking
   chocolate, chopped
1/2 c. water
3/4 c. sugar

1/8 t. salt
1/2 c. whipping cream,
   whipped
6 c. hot milk

Melt chocolate in a double boiler over medium heat. Add water; stir constantly for 4 minutes. Add sugar and salt; cook 4 minutes longer, stirring constantly. Let cool; fold in whipped cream. To serve, place a heaping tablespoon of chocolate mixture into each serving cup and pour about one cup hot milk on top, or until cup is almost filled. Stir lightly to blend. Serves 8.

For a cheery winter welcome, fill a child's wagon with poinsettias and vintage ornaments and place by the front door.

Nighty-Night Cocoa

4 1-oz. sqs. semi-sweet
   baking chocolate,
   chopped
4 1-oz. sqs. bittersweet
   baking chocolate,
   chopped

1/3 c. brown sugar, packed
2 c. whipping cream
2 c. milk
1 t. vanilla extract

Melt chocolates and brown sugar in a double boiler over
medium heat. Gradually whisk in whipping cream and milk
until frothy and heated through. Remove from heat; stir in
vanilla. Serves 4.

The first fall of snow is not only an event,
it is a magical event.
-J.B. Priestley

Sweet Dreams Hot Chocolate

1 c. milk
chocolate syrup to taste
1/2 t. vanilla extract

1/4 t. cinnamon
Garnish: mini marshmallows

Warm milk in a small saucepan over low heat, taking care
not to scorch. As milk is warming, stir in chocolate syrup,
vanilla and cinnamon with a small whisk; do not beat. When
syrup has dissolved, pour into a mug; top with marshmallows.
Makes one serving.

Peppy Peppermint Hot Chocolate

1 T. semi-sweet chocolate
    chips
1-oz. pkg. hot chocolate mix

3/4 c. boiling water
Garnish: peppermint candy
    cane

Place chocolate chips in a mug; add hot chocolate mix and
boiling water. Stir with candy cane. Makes one serving.

Spend a wintry evening with your family...just being
together. Put on your jammies, build a fire,
sip creamy cocoa and enjoy the twinkling lights
and frosty windowpanes!

★ Classics ★

Grammy's Best Hot Chocolate Mix

4-lb. pkg. powdered milk
2 15-oz. pkgs. chocolate
    drink mix
2 16-oz. pkgs. powdered
    sugar
16-oz. jar powdered
    non-dairy creamer

2 3.9-oz. pkgs. instant
    chocolate pudding mix
10-1/2 oz. pkg. mini
    marshmallows

Combine all ingredients in a very large container; mix well.
Pour into three, one-gallon airtight containers. Seal tightly
and attach instructions. Makes about 3 gallons.

Instructions:

Place about 1/3 cup mix into a mug. Add one cup boiling
water; stir to dissolve. Makes one serving.

Fill an old-fashioned milk bottle with cocoa mix...look for
them at flea markets and antique shops.

Hot Chocolate Malt Mix

25-oz. pkg. powdered milk
16-oz. jar powdered non-
    dairy creamer
13-oz. jar malted milk
    powder

16-oz. jar hot chocolate mix
1 c. powdered sugar
1 t. vanilla powder
2 c. mini marshmallows

Use a wire whisk to combine all ingredients. Divide mix equally into 4 plastic zipping bags and attach instructions to each. Makes about 13 cups.

Instructions:

Place 3 tablespoons mix into a mug. Add one cup boiling water; stir well. Makes one serving.

HᴑT
CHOCOLATE
MaLt MIX

Place 3 tablespoons mix into a mug. Add 1 cup boiling water & stir well. Makes 1 serving.

Here's your instruction tag to copy & tie on.

Bavarian Mint Mocha Mix

1/4 c. powdered non-dairy
   creamer
1/3 c. powdered sugar

1/4 c. instant coffee granules
2 T. baking cocoa
3 peppermint candies

Combine all ingredients in a blender or food processor. Blend until candies are finely ground. Pour into a one-quart, wide-mouth canning jar; seal tightly. Attach instructions. Makes about one cup.

Instructions:

Place 2 to 3 rounded tablespoons mix into a mug. Add one cup boiling water; stir to dissolve. Makes one serving.

The simplest things can make any gift special. Spray paint a coffee can red, line with homespun and tuck a jar of cocoa mix inside. Add a wide length of homespun around the middle of the can and knot, then glue a whimsical wooden gingerbread man over the knot.

What-a-Parade Cocoa Mix

1/2 c. sugar
2 T. whole almonds
1-oz. sq. bittersweet baking
   chocolate, chopped

1/4 c. baking cocoa
1/2 t. vanilla powder
1 t. cinnamon
1/2 t. ground cloves

Place sugar and almonds in a food processor; process until almonds are finely ground. Add remaining ingredients; process until mixture is finely ground. Store in an airtight container; attach instructions. Makes one cup.

Instructions:

Add one tablespoon mix into a mug. Add one cup hot milk; whisk until frothy. Makes one serving.

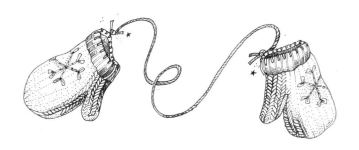

Slip a cocoa mix inside a new thermos and tie on some
mittens...a clever gift for a winter celebration.

Classics

Cozy Homemade Hot Cocoa Mix

32-oz. pkg. chocolate drink
   mix
16-oz. jar powdered
   non-dairy creamer
16-oz. pkg. powdered sugar

8-oz. pkg. powdered milk
2 6-oz. pkgs. mini
   semi-sweet chocolate
   chips

Combine ingredients in a large bowl; mix well. Store in an
airtight container; attach instructions.

Instructions:

Place 3 to 4 heaping tablespoons mix into one cup boiling
water; stir until chocolate chips are melted. Makes one serving.

Scoop cocoa mix into a plastic icing cone and fill
any extra space at the top with mini marshmallows...
what a fun stocking stuffer!

Puffy Homemade Marshmallows

4 envs. unflavored gelatin
3/4 c. water
3 c. sugar
1-1/4 c. light corn syrup

1/4 t. salt
2 t. vanilla extract
1-1/2 c. powdered sugar, divided

Spray a 13"x9" baking pan with non-stick cooking spray. Line with wax paper; spray with cooking spray and set aside. Sprinkle gelatin into water in a medium bowl; let stand for 5 minutes. Combine sugar, corn syrup, salt and vanilla in a heavy saucepan; bring to a boil. Cook over high heat until mixture reaches the soft-ball stage, 234 to 243 degrees on a candy thermometer. Using an electric mixer on high speed, beat hot mixture slowly into gelatin mixture until very stiff, about 10 minutes. Pour into prepared pan; smooth top with a spatula. Let stand overnight, uncovered, until firm. Invert baking pan on a surface sprinkled with one cup powdered sugar; peel off wax paper. Cut into desired shapes using a sharp knife or cookie cutters sprayed with cooking spray. Roll cut sides in remaining powdered sugar. Store in an airtight container at room temperature for up to 3 weeks. Makes about 2 dozen.

Decorate a paper sack with rubber stamps and fill with Puffy Homemade Marshmallows. Fold over the top, punch 2 holes and slide a peppermint stick through for a sweet gift bag.

Spiced Hot Cocoa Mix

1 vanilla bean
1-1/3 c. sugar
1-1/3 c. powdered milk
1 c. baking cocoa

3 T. instant espresso powder
1/2 t. cinnamon
1/4 t. vanilla powder
1/8 t. ground cardamom

Split vanilla bean; scrape seeds and place in a medium bowl, discarding shell. Add sugar; stir to blend. Add remaining ingredients; mix well. Spoon into an airtight container and attach instructions. Makes about 3-1/2 cups.

Instructions:

Place 1/4 cup mix into a mug. Add one cup boiling water; stir to dissolve. Makes one serving.

Cooler weather and longer evenings are a cozy time just right for curling up with a good book. Keep several of your favorites on a table next to a comfy chair, make yourself a cup of hot cocoa and sit back to enjoy.

Merry Mocha Cappuccino Mix

1-1/4 c. powdered non-dairy creamer
6 T. plus 2 t. instant espresso powder
1/2 c. plus 2 T. powdered sugar
3 T. plus 1 t. baking cocoa
2 t. cinnamon

Combine all ingredients; mix well and pour into an airtight container. Seal tightly; attach instructions. Makes about 2-1/2 cups.

Instructions:

Place 4 tablespoons mix into a mug. Add one cup boiling water; stir to dissolve. Makes one serving.

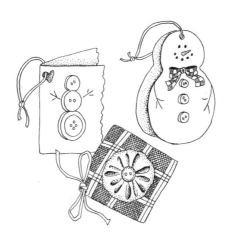

Handmade gift tags are perfect for homemade cocoa mixes. Use cookie cutters as patterns...just trace around a snowman, cut out and add the finishing touches! Dress up your tags with vintage buttons or yo-yos.

Classics

Raspberry Hot Cocoa Mix

2 c. powdered sugar
1 c. baking cocoa
1 c. non-dairy powdered
    creamer
1/2 t. salt

3 .15-oz. pkgs.
    unsweetened raspberry
    drink mix
5-1/2 c. powdered milk

Combine all ingredients in a gallon-size plastic zipping bag;
shake to combine. Place in an airtight container; attach
instructions. Makes 9 cups mix.

Instructions:

Place 3 tablespoons mix into a mug. Add one cup boiling
water; stir to dissolve. Makes one serving.

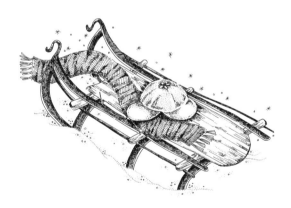

Throw an impromptu sledding party for the first
snowfall...gather with friends & neighbors to enjoy
some fun and then head back home for
a cozy fire and hot cocoa.

French Vanilla Cocoa Mix

10-1/2 c. powdered milk
16-oz. pkg. powdered sugar
2 8-oz. jars French vanilla-
   flavored powdered
   non-dairy creamer
3-1/2 c. hot chocolate mix
2-3/4 c. powdered non-dairy
   creamer
1/2 t. salt

Combine all ingredients in a large bowl; mix well. Divide
evenly into eight, one-quart wide-mouth canning jars.
Seal tightly; attach instructions. Makes 8 jars.

Instructions:

Place 2 to 3 heaping tablespoons mix into a mug. Add one cup
hot milk or boiling water; stir to dissolve. Makes one serving.

Spoon homemade cocoa mix into plastic zipping bags and
tuck into holiday mugs. Keep several in a basket by the
door...so handy as gifts for drop-in guests.

Mocha-Mint Meltaway Mix

2 c. rich hot cocoa mix   1/4 t. peppermint extract
1/4 c. instant coffee granules   1/4 t. vanilla powder

Place all ingredients in a blender; process until powdered.
Spoon into an airtight jar; attach instructions. Makes
2-1/4 cups.

Instructions:

Place 3 tablespoons mix into a mug. Add one cup hot milk or
boiling water; stir until dissolved. Makes one serving.

Candy Cane Stirrers

6-oz. pkg. semi-sweet   48 mini peppermint
  chocolate chips, divided   candy canes

Place chips in a small microwave-safe bowl. Microwave on
high setting for one minute; stir until smooth. Microwave for
an additional 10 to 20 seconds; stir until smooth. Set bowl in
a pan of hot water to keep chocolate soft, making sure water
does not mix with chocolate. Dip straight end of each candy
cane into chocolate to coat; lay on wax paper to cool. Wrap
each candy cane in clear plastic wrap. Makes 48 stirrers.

Ah! There is nothing like staying home
for real comfort.

-Jane Austen

Marshmallow Cocoa Mix

25-oz. pkg. powdered milk
1-1/2 c. powdered non-dairy
   creamer

3 c. hot chocolate mix
1-1/2 c. powdered sugar
2 c. mini marshmallows

Combine ingredients; mix well. Divide mix equally into four, one-quart jars. Attach instructions to each. Makes 4 jars.

Instructions:

Place 1/2 cup mix into a mug. Add one cup boiling water; stir to dissolve. Makes one serving.

Remember all the nice things that go along with
making someone feel better...crossword puzzles,
a book by a favorite author, a box
of tissues and a big jar of cocoa mix.

Cheery Cherry Hot Cocoa Mix

3/4 c. hot chocolate mix
.13-oz. pkg. unsweetened
   cherry drink mix

4 cherry-flavored licorice
   twists

Combine first 2 ingredients in a plastic zipping bag; shake to mix. Wrap licorice twists in plastic wrap; attach to mix along with instructions. Makes about one cup.

Instructions:

Place 3 tablespoons mix into a mug. Add 3/4 cup boiling water; stir well with one licorice twist. Makes one serving.

A morning surprise! Leave a mug filled with cocoa mix on a co-worker's desk for her to enjoy when she arrives.

White Hot Cocoa Mix

1 c. white chocolate chips   2 t. vanilla powder
1/4 c. mini marshmallows   2 t. orange zest

Combine all ingredients; place in a small airtight container.
Attach instructions. Makes about 1-1/4 cups.

Instructions:

Combine 3/4 cup milk and 2 tablespoons mix in a small heavy
saucepan over medium heat. Whisk well until chocolate is
melted and smooth. Makes one serving.

Nothing's better on a snow day than building a snowman.
Keep a box filled with everything the kids need...mittens,
scarf, hat and buttons. Don't forget a camera too.
There's sure to be lots of fun!

Minty Hot Cocoa Mix

1-1/4 c. powdered milk
1/4 c. hot chocolate mix
1/4 c. mint chocolate chips
1 t. cinnamon

2 T. chocolate-flavored
   powdered non-dairy
   creamer

Mix all ingredients well and pour into a one-pint jar. Attach a gift tag with instructions. Makes 2 cups.

Instructions:

Place 1/3 cup mix into a mug; add one cup boiling water. Stir until mint chips are melted. Makes one serving.

Invite friends & neighbors over for an old-fashioned tree-trimming party! Pull out all your favorite ornaments, have holiday music playing and serve lots of yummy snacks.

Chocolate Stirring Spoons

6-oz. pkg. semi-sweet
    chocolate chips
1 t. shortening

24 plastic spoons
3/4 c. white chocolate chips
Optional: candy sprinkles

Line baking sheets with parchment; set aside. Place chocolate chips in a small microwave-safe bowl. Microwave on high setting for one minute; stir until smooth. Microwave for an additional 10 to 20 seconds. Add shortening; stir until smooth. Set bowl in a pan of hot water to keep chocolate soft, making sure water does not mix with chocolate. Dip bowls of spoons into chocolate to coat; place on baking sheets to cool. Place white chips in a heavy plastic zipping bag; microwave on high for 30 to 45 seconds. Knead bag; microwave an additional 10 seconds; knead until smooth. Snip a tiny corner from bag; squeeze to drizzle over spoons. If desired, decorate immediately with candy sprinkles. Cool. Makes 24 spoons.

Friends will love their cocoa breaks with Chocolate
Stirring Spoons! Fill a tin cup or a small vase with
mini candies and insert the spoon handles, so the spoons
stand up. Wrap with clear cellophane, gather ends at
the top and tie with a pretty ribbon.

Iced Chocolate

3 c. chocolate syrup
2 qts. milk
2 t. vanilla extract
2 pts. whipping cream

crushed ice
Garnish: additional whipped
    cream, maraschino
    cherries

Blend chocolate syrup, milk and vanilla in a large bowl; set aside. Whip cream until thick; add to chocolate mixture. Blend until light and frothy. Pour into serving glasses half-filled with crushed ice. Top with a dollop of whipped cream and a cherry. Makes 18 servings.

Throw a "Christmas in July" crafting party with girlfriends and serve refreshing Iced Chocolate. Chocolate beverages are too yummy to save for cold weather!

Biscotti Cookies

1/2 c. oil
3 eggs
1 c. sugar
1 T. almond or anise extract
3-1/4 c. all-purpose flour

1 T. baking powder
Optional: chocolate chips,
  melted, or powdered
  sugar glaze

Beat together oil, eggs, sugar and extract in a medium bowl until well blended; set aside. Combine flour and baking powder; stir into oil mixture until dough forms. Divide dough in half. With floured hands, form each half into a long roll on a greased baking sheet. Flatten each roll to 1/2-inch thick. Bake at 375 degrees for 18 to 25 minutes, until golden. Cool on a wire rack. When just cool enough to handle, slice rolls crosswise, 1/2-inch thick, with a pizza cutter or knife. Return to baking sheet, cut-side up. Bake for 6 to 10 minutes, until lightly toasted; turn slices over and bake until lightly toasted on other side. Cool on a wire rack. If desired, drizzle with melted chocolate or powdered sugar glaze. Makes 2 dozen.

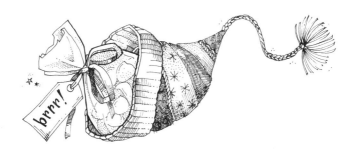

Slip homemade Biscotti Cookies inside a woolly
toboggan...perfect for a holiday gift swap and
just right for dunking in hot cocoa!

SNOWMAN SOUP

COLD HANDS WARM HEARTS!

Place the following ingredients in a plastic
zipping bag and attach the tag...

    1-oz. pkg. hot cocoa mix
    1 candy cane
    2 T. mini marshmallows
    1 milk chocolate drop

SNOWMAN SOUP

Santa says you've been good this year...
I'm always glad to hear it!
With freezing weather drawing near,
You'll need to warm the spirit!
Here's a little Snowman Soup,
Complete with stirring stick.
Add hot water and sip it slow...
It's sure to do the trick!

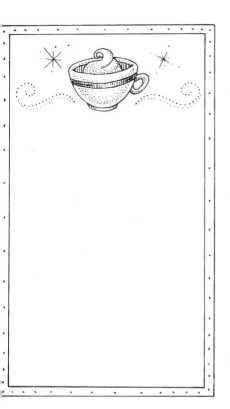

Tags for your gift mixes!

to:

from:

1. Copy 2. Color 3. Cut out 4. Share

Checklist for
"Who Wouldn't LOVE A
Cocoa Mix as a Gift?"

- ☐ _____
- ☐ _____
- ☐ _____
- ☐ _____
- ☐ _____
- ☐ _____
- ☐ _____

from our house to yours

Index